Counselors

ABDO
Publishing Company

A Buddy **Book by**
Julie Murray

VISIT US AT
www.abdopublishing.com

Published by ABDO Publishing Company, 8000 West 78th Street, Edina, Minnesota 55439.

Printed in the United States of America, North Mankato, Minnesota.
022010
092010

 PRINTED ON RECYCLED PAPER

Coordinating Series Editor: Rochelle Baltzer
Editor: Sarah Tieck
Contributing Editors: Heidi M.D. Elston, Megan M. Gunderson, BreAnn Rumsch,
    Marcia Zappa
Graphic Design: Maria Hosley
Cover Photograph: *Photo Researchers, Inc.*: ©Spencer Grant.
Interior Photographs/Illustrations: *Alamy*: Jeff Greenberg (p. 21), Dennis MacDonald (p. 7),
    Stock Connection Blue (p. 27); *AP Photo*: Mel Evans (p. 15), Marc Lester/Anchorage
    Daily News (p. 15), Samuel Peebles/Daily Citizen (p. 9), Matt Ryerson/The Hawk Eye
    (p. 23), Marcio Jose Sanchez (p. 5), Phil Sandlin (p. 30), Rogelio Solis (pp. 11, 27);
    Corbis: ©Will & Deni McIntyre (pp. 17, 19); *Getty Images*: Joseph Scherschel/Time
    Life Pictures (p. 25); *iStockphoto*: ©iStockphoto.com/sjlocke (p. 13); *Photolibrary*: Alex
    Mares-Manton (p. 29); *Shutterstock*: KK Art and Photography (p. 5).

Library of Congress Cataloging-in-Publication Data

Murray, Julie, 1969-
  Counselors / Julie Murray.
    p. cm. -- (Going to work : school edition)
  ISBN 978-1-61613-505-8
  1. Educational counseling--Juvenile literature. 2. Student counselors--Juvenile literature. I.
Title.
  LB1027.5.M86 2011
  371.4--dc22

                                                                                    2009050818

Contents

People at Work

Going to work is an important part of life. At work, people use their skills to complete tasks and earn money.

There are many different types of workplaces. Schools, factories, and offices are all workplaces.

Some counselors work in schools. They listen to students, answer questions, and help with problems. This is meaningful work.

A counselor works with many different students in a school.

Office Visit

School counselors usually have their own offices. There, they meet with students and give them advice. Counselors help students with school and personal problems.

Students may set a meeting time or just stop by their counselor's office.

7

For school counselors, every day is different. Many begin work before the school day starts. They may walk the hallways and talk to students.

Sometimes, students have problems with other students. Other times, they have trouble with family members. Counselors help students with these problems so they can succeed in school.

Counselors spend time in areas where students gather. This helps them get to know students.

Working Together

School counselors work with many people every day. They talk to students, teachers, principals, and parents. Counselors answer their phone calls and meet with them.

Counselors visit classrooms. They talk about getting along with others. They teach students how to meet **goals**. And, they help teachers plan some lessons.

School counselors visit classrooms to work with students in small groups.

Job Training

A school counselor must have a college **degree**. To earn the degree, he or she studies education or **psychology**. Most states also require an advanced degree.

During college, counselors learn how to work with students. Before earning their degrees, many practice their skills in schools.

When people earn degrees, they attend a graduation ceremony. This special event honors their hard work.

Some people work as teachers before becoming school counselors.

Did You Know?

13

A school counselor must get a license from his or her state. Every state has different laws to decide who works with students. Some states have social workers or psychologists in schools.

School counselors work in elementary, middle, and high schools. Some states require different licenses for each age group.

Life Helpers

Students meet with school counselors alone or in small groups. They share their feelings. Counselors offer helpful advice.

Counselors may hold small group meetings in their offices. This connects students with others who have the same problems.

Counselors help students with many different problems. They talk them through family changes, such as a new brother or sister. They help students set learning **goals**. And, they help students get along with each other.

School counselors keep what students say private. But if laws are being broken, they must share what they know.

Counselors are trusted to **protect** students. They must notify officials if a person is in danger.

Many times, counselors meet one-on-one with students.

Class Work

School counselors help students become good citizens. So, they may teach classes on building character.

When students build character, they learn to respect others and make good choices. They also learn to be caring, fair, and trustworthy.

Counselors teach lessons that help students learn about themselves.

Did You Know?

Therapy dogs are pets that help people learn, heal, and connect with others. They also comfort people and cheer them up.

School counselors also work with students who have special needs. Counselors teach them life skills. This helps them succeed in school and at home.

Sometimes, students and their families need more help. School social workers or **psychologists** may provide further help.

Counselors may use therapy dogs to help students who have special needs.

HISTORY LESSON

U.S. schools started counseling students in the early 1900s. They mostly helped high school students prepare for jobs.

In the 1960s, school counselors began to help students build character. They taught social skills and other life skills.

Long ago, counselors prepared girls and boys for different jobs. Today, men and women have the same job opportunities.

Today, school counselors work with students of all ages. Counselors help them improve behavior and build character.

Modern classrooms may be full and busy. School counselors are often able to give extra attention to students. This helps prevent problems and aids in learning.

Some counselors have special tools in their office. Toys and other objects help them work with students.

Helpful Workers

School counselors listen to and help students. They often improve their lives. This is important work that benefits the community.

Many students think of a school counselor as a helper and a friend.

The School News

Teachers as Counselors

Jesse B. Davis was a high school principal in the early 1900s. He asked teachers to help students prepare for life and work. This was one of the first U.S. counseling programs.

Honoring Counselors

National School Counseling Week takes place in February in the United States. School counselors have been honored this way since the late 1990s.

Important Words

degree a title given by a college to its students for completing their studies. An advanced degree, such as a master's or a doctorate, is earned by completing graduate school after college.

goal something that a person works to reach or complete.

license (LEYE-suhnts) a paper or a card showing that someone is allowed to do something by law.

protect (pruh-TEHKT) to guard against harm or danger.

psychology (seye-KAHL-uh-jee) the science of the mind and behavior. A person who works with people's minds and behaviors is a psychologist.

Web Sites

To learn more about counselors, visit ABDO Publishing Company online. Web sites about counselors are featured on our Book Links page. These links are routinely monitored and updated to provide the most current information available.

www.abdopublishing.com

Index